Distant Stars and Asteroids

A Kid's Guide to the Mysteries of Outer Space

Children's Astronomy & Space Books

pfiffikus
EDUCATIONAL BOOKS FOR CHILDREN K-12

Copyright 2016

Aside from the planets, our Solar System is also home to other interesting objects! Read on and learn about some of them.

Asteroids are
rocks that
orbit around
the Sun.

Asteroids are also called planetoids or minor planets.

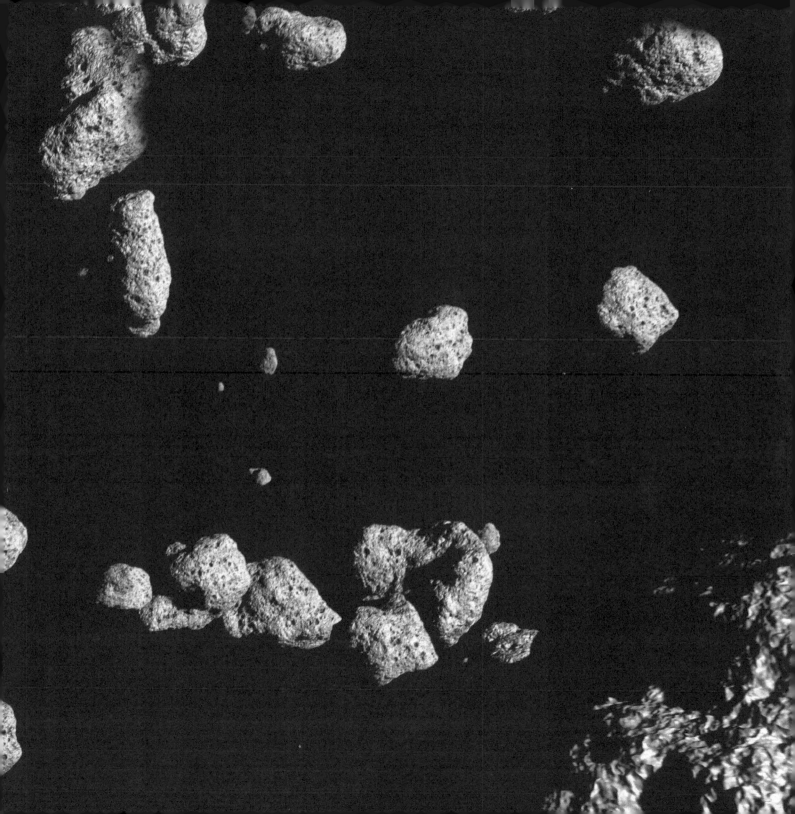

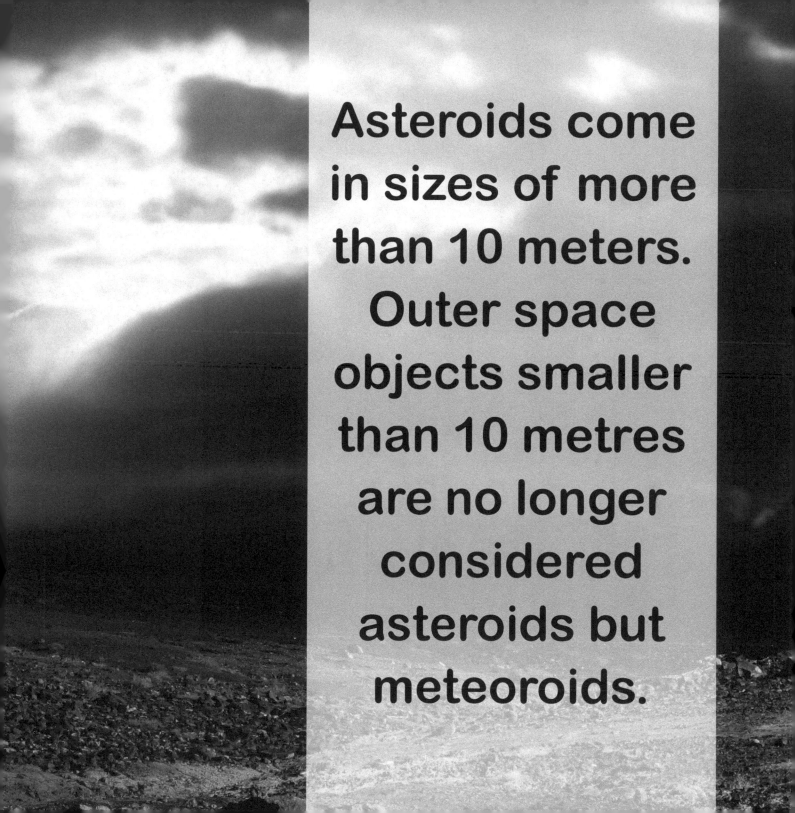

Asteroids come in sizes of more than 10 meters. Outer space objects smaller than 10 metres are no longer considered asteroids but meteoroids.

Ceres was the first asteroid discovered. It was discovered in 1801 by Giuseppe Piazzi.

Ceres has a diameter of 950 kilometres and is now considered a dwarf planet.

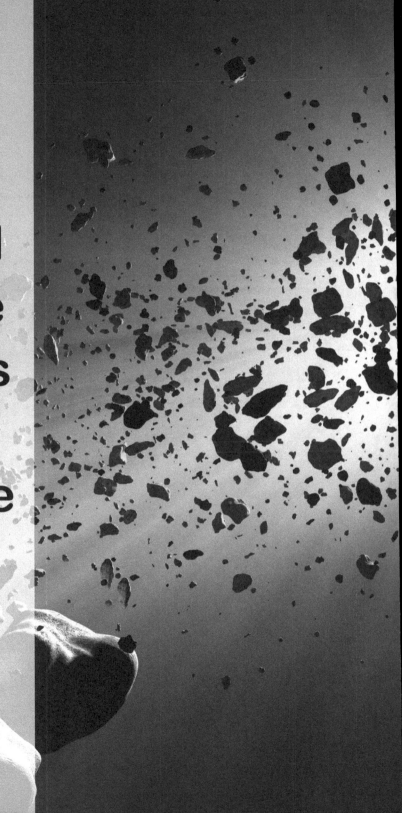

An asteroid belt is found between the planets Mars and Jupiter. This is where you can find Ceres.

Asteroids do not have enough gravity to pull themselves together and form planets.

There are 26 known large asteroids and countless small asteroids.

It is believed that asteroids are the reasons why dinosaurs no longer exist.

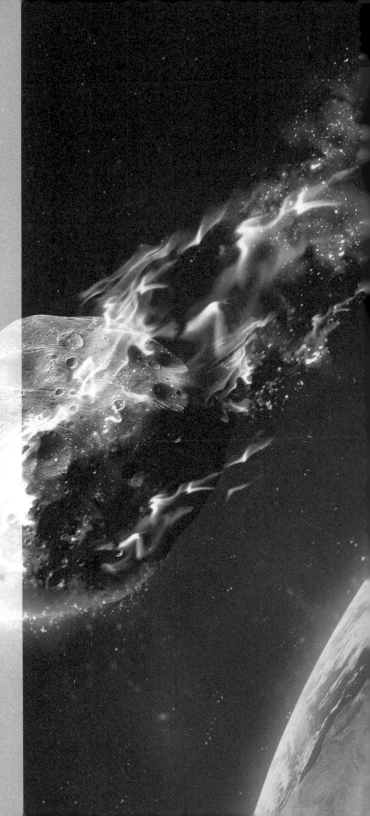

The largest
known
asteroid is
the Quaoar. It
is one-tenth
the size of
the Earth.

When asteroids crash, thousands of small pieces are chipped off and pulled into planets. They then become known as meteors.

Another class
of objects
found in the
Solar System
are stars.

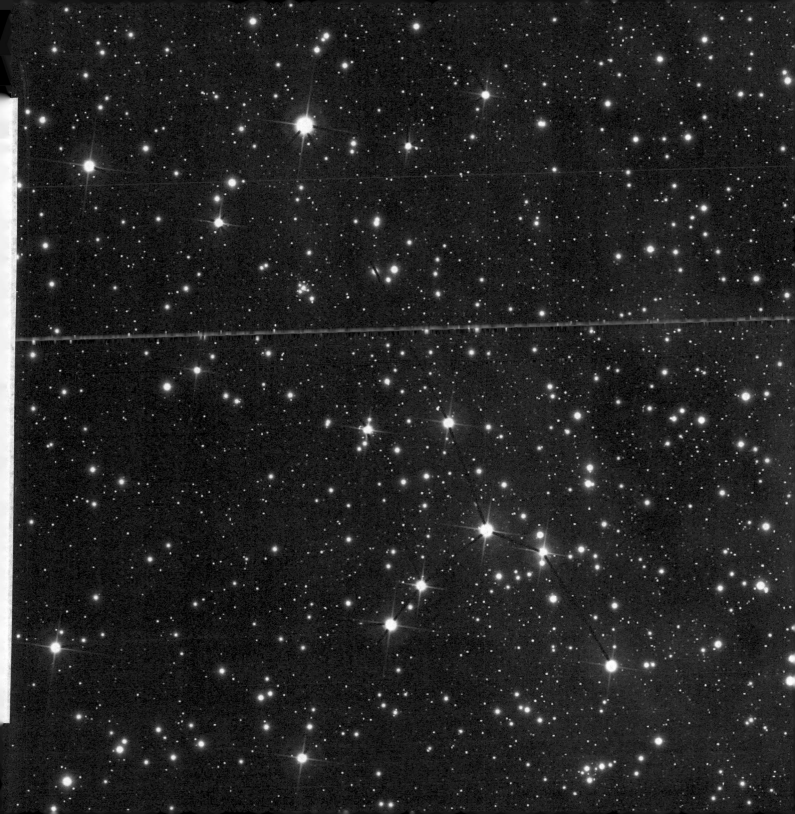

A star is a big bright sphere of hot gas. It has its own gravity so it can't be pulled into planets.

Did you know
that our Sun
is also a star?
It is classified
as a yellow
dwarf star and
is the nearest
star to Earth.

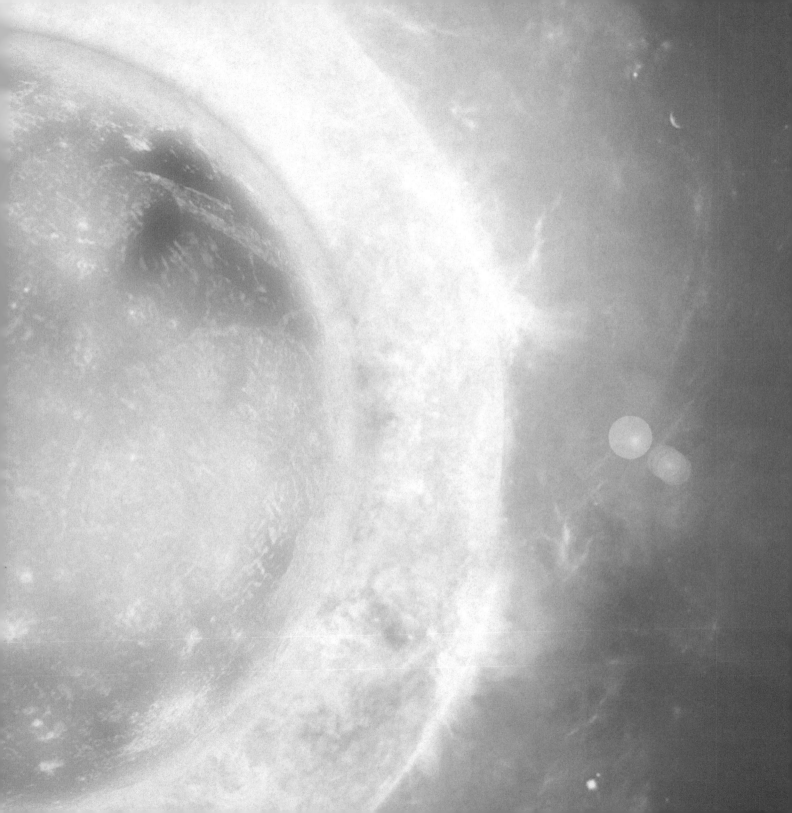

Stars are different colors depending on how hot they are. They can be brown, red, orange, yellow, white or blue. The hottest star is blue while the coolest star is red.

Stars are said to be between 1 and 10 billion years old.

There are over 200 billion stars in our galaxy.

What outer space object would you like to study in the future? Research and have fun!